GOD IS BETTER THAN

Princesses

SARAH REJU
ILLUSTRATED BY
ROGER DE KLERK

Do you love princesses? Princesses are amazing,
but God is better than princesses!

The birth of a princess is **announced** with fireworks, but God announced the birth of his Son, Jesus, with angels. God is better than princesses!
"…suddenly there was … a multitude of the heavenly host praising God…" Luke 2:13

A princess is beautiful, but her **beauty** is flawed and lasts only a short while. God is perfectly holy, without stain or sin forever. God is better than princesses!

"...Holy, holy, holy is the LORD of hosts; the whole earth is full of his glory!"
Isaiah 6:3

A princess may grow up to be crowned queen, but when she dies another queen will be crowned. God is King of kings forever. God is better than princesses!

"The Lord is king forever and ever..."
Psalm 10:16

A princess has fun *dancing* at the royal ball, but God rejoices when his people turn to him. God is better than princesses!

"…as the bridegroom rejoices over the bride, so shall your God rejoice over you." Isaiah 62:5

A princess has an **empire** that will one day break apart. Her servants will scatter. But God's people serve him for ever. His kingdom will never end. God is better than princesses!

"...a great multitude that no one could number...are before the throne of God, and serve him day and night in his temple..."
Revelation 7:9, 15

A princess has a *fort* that may crumble and fail to keep her safe, but trusting Jesus brings perfect safety and peace. God is better than princesses!

"The LORD of hosts is with us; the God of Jacob is our fortress." Psalm 46:7

A princess wears a beautiful *gown*, but God is clothed with majesty, splendor, and glory. God is better than princesses!

"...O LORD my God, you are very great! You are clothed with splendor and majesty, covering yourself with light as with a garment..." Psalm 104:1-2

A princess can live *happily* ever after only to the end of her life. God gives his people a life full of joy with him forever in heaven. God is better than princesses!

"God will wipe away every tear from their eyes, and death shall be no more, neither shall there be mourning, nor crying, nor pain ..." Revelation 21:4

A fairy tale princess has a life and world that are *imaginary*, but God is real. God is better than princesses!

"In the beginning, God created the heavens and the earth."
Genesis 1:1

A princess has a crown that sparkles with *jewels*, but God shines brighter than the sun. God is better than princesses!

"...They will need no light of lamp or sun, for the Lord God will be their light..."
Revelation 22:5

A princess will inherit a **kingdom** of castles and lands, but God is king of the whole universe forever. God is better than princesses!

"Yours, O LORD, is the greatness and the power and the glory and the victory and the majesty, for all that is in the heavens and in the earth is yours ... you rule over all." 1 Chronicles 29:11-12

A princess *loves* the handsome prince, who loves her in return. However, God loves people who hate him, and he sent his Son, Jesus Christ, to die for them. God is better than princesses!

"...God shows his love for us in that while we were still sinners, Christ died for us."
Romans 5:8

A princess gets *married* to a prince, but this ends when they die. God's marriage to his people will last forever. God is better than princesses!

"Let us rejoice and exult and give him the glory, for the marriage of the Lamb has come..." Revelation 19:7

A princess lacks *nothing*. Her life is full of beauty and comfort, but God made himself nothing by becoming a man. He suffered and died in our place. God is better than princesses!

"[Christ Jesus]... made himself nothing... he humbled himself by becoming obedient to the point of death, even death on a cross."
Philippians 2:7-8

A princess story begins with *"once upon a time,"* because it didn't really happen, but God's Word is true and can be trusted. God is better than princesses!

"...these words are trustworthy and true."
Revelation 21:5

A princess lives in a sparkling *palace*, but God is not limited to one place. God is everywhere. God is better than princesses!

"The God who made the world and everything in it, being Lord of heaven and earth, does not live in temples made by man." Acts 17:24

One day, a princess will become a powerful queen, but God already has all the power and authority. God is better than princesses!

"...the surpassing power belongs to God and not to us." 2 Corinthians 4:7

A princess might share a few of her golden *riches* with her subjects, but God heaps his riches of grace, mercy, and salvation on his people.
God is better than princesses!

In him we have redemption through his blood, the forgiveness of sins, in accordance with the riches of God's grace that he lavished on us. Ephesians 1:7-8

A princess holds the royal *scepter*, but she sometimes makes bad decisions.
God is the perfect judge who always does what is right.
God is better than princesses!

"...Your throne, O God, is forever and ever, the scepter of uprightness is the scepter of your kingdom." Hebrews 1:8

A princess sits on her *throne* and judges her subjects. God's throne is heaven itself, and he judges the entire earth. God is better than princesses!

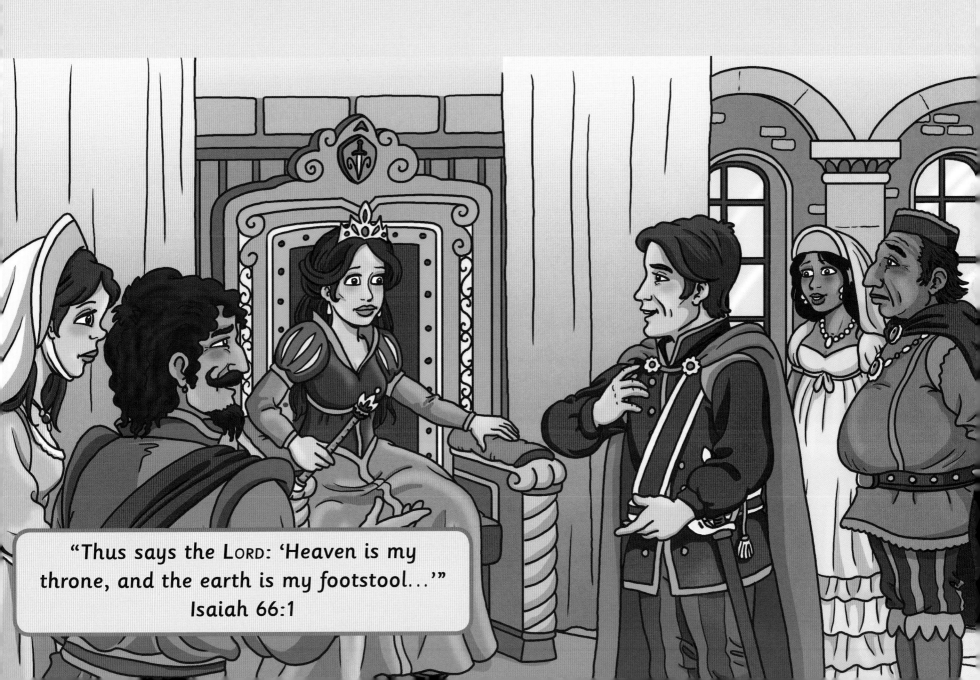

"Thus says the LORD: 'Heaven is my throne, and the earth is my footstool...'"
Isaiah 66:1

A princess is *upper class*. Her servants help her with everything. Jesus came to be a servant and give his life for his people. God is better than princesses!

"For even the Son of Man came not to be served but to serve, and to give his life as a ransom for many."
Mark 10:45

A princess can often be **vain**, spending lots of time and energy making herself beautiful, but God sees the heart, and he knows what is really in a person. God is better than princesses!

"...For the LORD sees not as man sees: man looks on the outward appearance, but the LORD looks on the heart."
1 Samuel 16:7

The *word* of a princess is law for a short time, but God created all things by the power of his Word. God is better than princesses.

"…the universe was created by the Word of God…" Hebrews 11:3

The subjects of a princess *eXalt* her by bowing or curtseying when they meet her.
When people meet God, they fall flat on their faces and worship him.
God is better than princesses!

"The twenty-four elders fall down before him who is seated on the throne and worship him who lives forever and ever. They cast their crowns before the throne..."
Revelation 4:10

A **young** princess has only lived a few years, but God lives forever. God is better than princesses!

"To the King of the ages, immortal, invisible, the only God, be honor and glory forever and ever. Amen." 1 Timothy 1:17

Even at the zenith and peak of her power, a princess cannot save her subjects from their sins. Only God can do that. God is better than princesses!

"...you shall call his name Jesus, for he will save his people from their sins."
Matthew 1:21

11

Princesses are beautiful, powerful, and rich!
But God is better than princesses!